This is a book of simple rhyme

With strange sounding words on every line

It's facts with fun I hope you'll find

But prose is poetry of a different kind

A mix of words that don't always match

Finding the rhythm, well that's the catch

Read me when you find the time

But remember, prose doesn't always rhyme

What other colour can bears be?

I'm lean, I'm mean, a killing machine
Head of the pride with a long golden mane
I have a strong wide jaw, and very sharp teeth
And when I'm hungry, I always eat meat
A gazelle or giraffe make a tasty treat
I lie in the grass looking out for my prey
Then I stalk them and leap but sometimes too late
They run for their lives what a lucky escape
My cubs I care for until they're full grown
Then send them out hunting for food of their own
I'm handsome; I'm sleek with a powerful physique
I'm a cat among cats; I'm king of the beasts

Can you find me?

Mud, mud, glorious mud, the song they sing is simple
But why lie in the sun when I can cool down my blood
In my wonderful watery hollow
I'm big and I'm heavy and wrinkly too
With a mouth that looks huge when I yawn
I have tiny eyes and ears each side of my nose
They can twirl independently, each, on their own
With my body submerged, I loll and I float
There I lie 'til I'm baked like a stone
At nightfall I graze on grassland nearby
Until full to the brim and too heavy to swim
On the banks of the river I lie down and doze

Can you find me?

What bird has a very long neck?

What bird can be black and white?

Slow, slow, never quick, just slow
Moving little and sleeping loads
I pass my time hanging out in the trees
I eat fruit and shoots and juicy leaves
My coat of grey has a greenish tinge
But it's just the algae that grow on me
Although I have a powerful grip
I can swim quite well if into the river I slip
I can turn my head two hundred degrees
So I can see all the things surrounding me
Central and South America is where I'm from
Deep in the rainforest is home sweet home

Can you find me?

I'm saggy and baggy and very dark grey
With a trunk that I swing as I go on my way
I'm the biggest land animal you'll ever see
I eat leaves from treetops, vegetarian, that's me
I travel in a herd across wide dusty plains
With my baby behind, holding on to my tail
My tusks are of ivory, white and precious
And men that are bad will hurt me to get it
Sometimes men capture me and bind me in chain
Making me work, ignoring my pain
When it's time to rest, I go down to the river
Raise my trunk in the air and create my own shower

Can you find me?

What other animal lives in a burrow?

What are baby kangaroos called?

I live in the Arctic with snow all around me
With glaciers that shimmer and ice on the sea
You will have to look hard to see me, you know
As my furry white coat blends well with the snow
I look very cuddly but don't be surprised
When I tell you I'm fierce and would eat you alive
I can swim really well in the freezing cold water
And I watch out for seals that I eat for my dinner
I have a shiny black nose that I sometimes cover
With my big white paw, so I'm not discovered.
I trek through the snow until I find the right spot
Then I lay myself down 'til the sun warms me up

Can you find me?

I have four legs and a tufted mane
A lion you say? Well think again
A nose that's black and lip that curls
Four hooves for feet and a swishy tail
Black and white stripes that are mine alone
Like fingerprints, no two the same
I'm related to the horsey types
But more distinctive with my unique stripes
I roam in a herd of a thousand or more
With my family close at hand
Looking out for lions and hyenas that laugh
They would eat me for dinner, if given the chance

Can you find me?

What animal looks like a hippopotamus but has a horn on its nose?

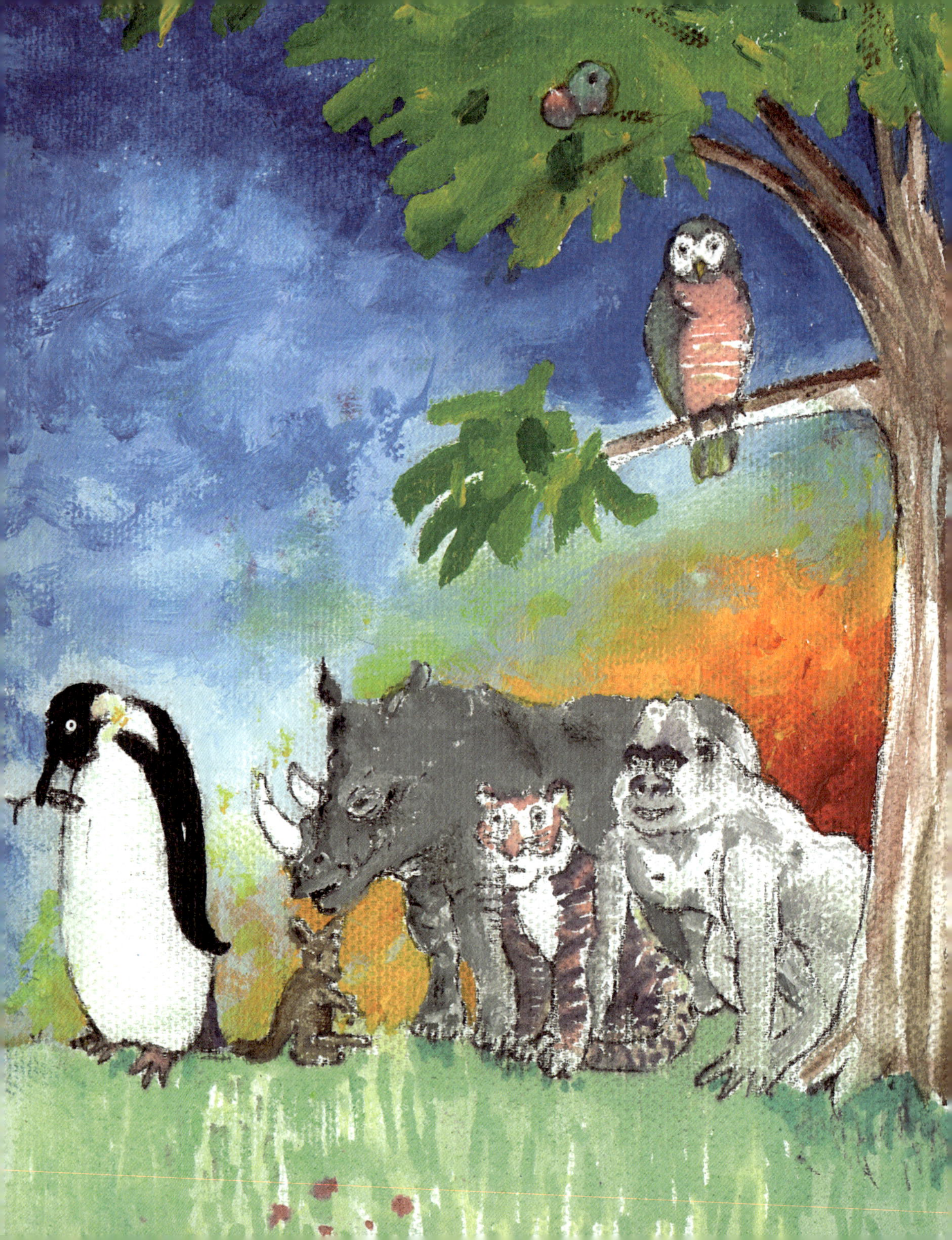

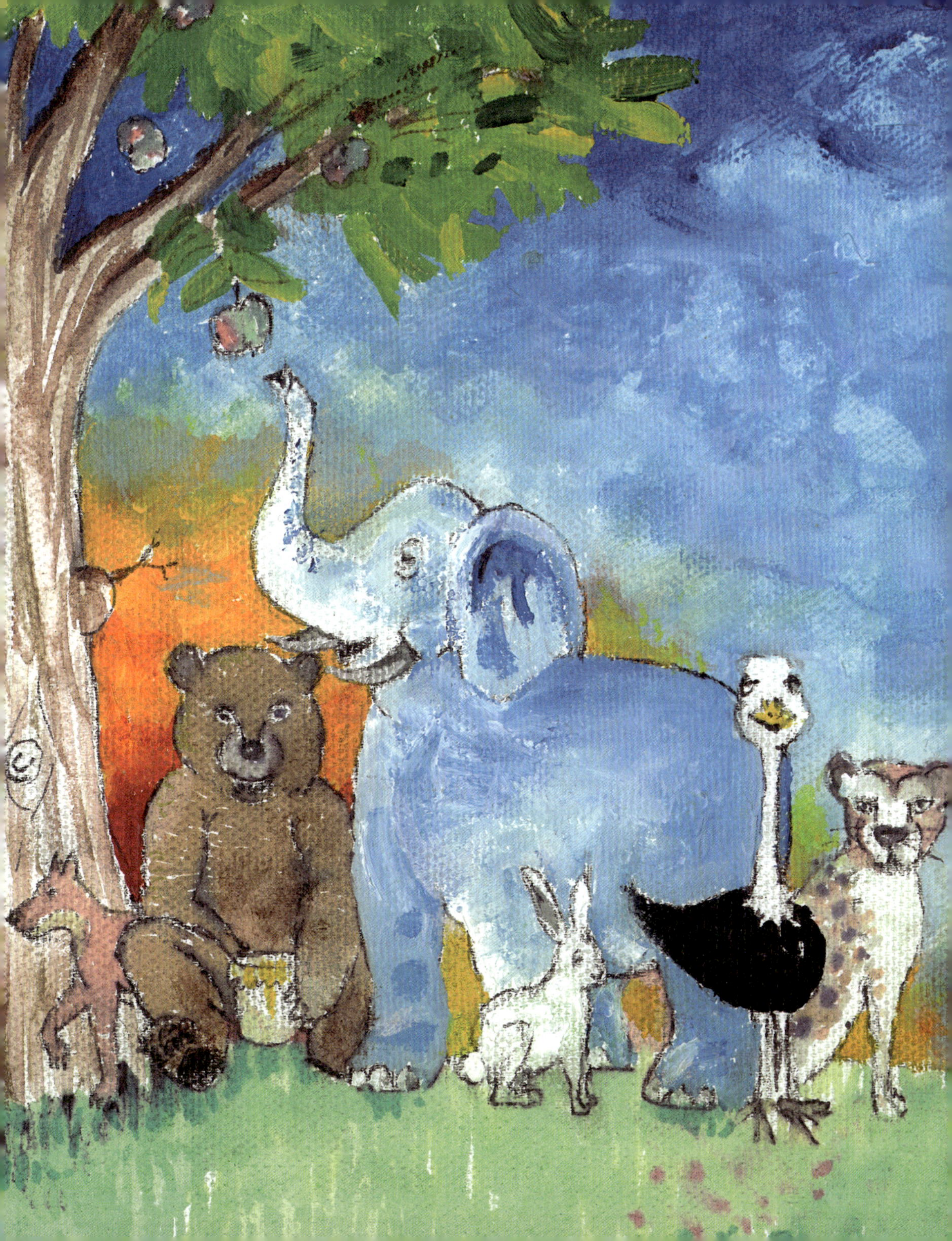

What very big animal looks like a monkey?

My! What a view I have over this land
I can see far in the distance from where I stand
I have a bony neck that is very long
With a pretty head and very long tongue
I stretch up to the sky reaching treetops high
Where the sweetest leaves on their branches lie
But drinking can be a quite a chore,
I have to spread my legs to reach the floor
My skin is patterned with funny shaped squares
Not straight at the edges but randomly there
I use it for camouflage, on my African trail
As a walk with a sway and a swish of my tail

Can you find me?

I love to hop from place to place
I've a spring in my step you see
With strong back legs and great big feet
I can jump very far, three metres each leap
I carry my young in a pouch on my tum
When first born they're just the size of a thumb
I stand on my hind legs when I'm ready to fight
Hit with my front feet, punching left, then right
A marsupial, I'm called, the biggest of all
When standing I can reach up to six feet or more
I'm an Australian 'roo, often found in the zoo
With my young peeping out over my pouch

Can you find me?

What other animal has a stripy coat?

What is the difference between an Indian and an African elephant?

I'm suricate of worldwide fame
But you may know me by a different name
I have a pointed face and crescent shaped ears
Long thin legs and very strong claws
I feast on insects, fruit and birds
And live in a burrow deep in the earth
Looking out for danger stand on guard
Like a sentry, there I stand for hours
With sharp barks and growls I raise the alarm
Sending friends scurrying away from harm
Finding a burrow they dive underground
And there they stay until the all clear sound

Can you find me?

I'm black and white and very round
I live in a country called China
Up in the trees or down on the ground
I'm happy wherever you find me
I spend all my days eating away
Delicious and tender bamboo shoots
I pick the branches with the pads of my feet
Stripping the cane with my very sharp teeth
I grind my food with a slide of my jaw
This way and that, until I am ready for more
Though not vegetarian I rarely eat meat
So you could say I'm one of the carnivore elite

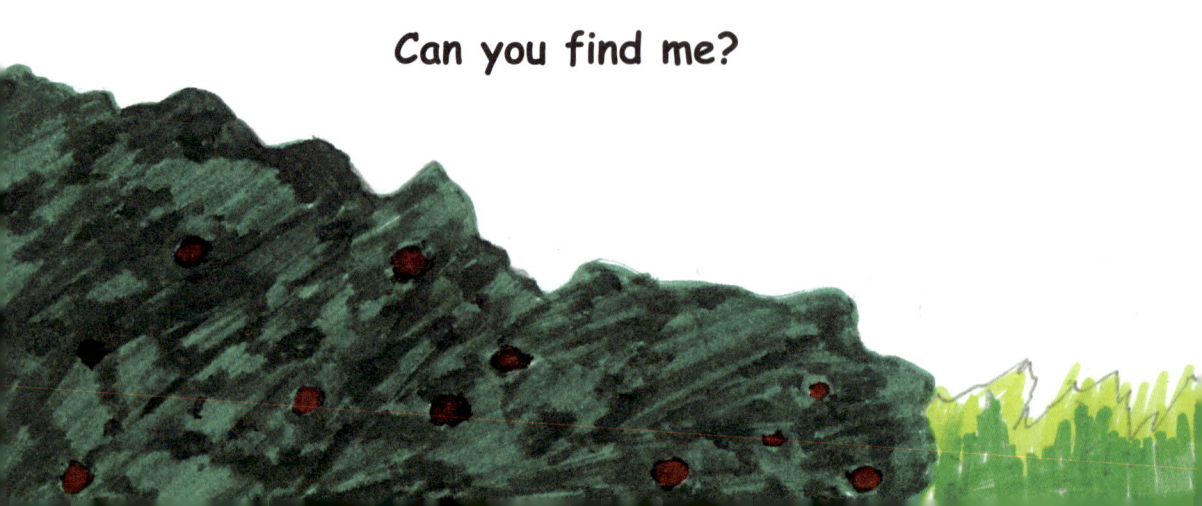

Can you find me?

What other animal lives in Australia?

What big wild cat has spots?

Swinging along from branch to branch
High in the treetops, by my very long arms
Hands on my wrists and hands for my feet
I have thumbs to hold on and help me to eat
Bananas, I love them and can peel with aplomb
Well, nobody eats them with the skin on
I'm furry all over. I can walk on two feet
I've a very wide mouth full of chattering teeth
I make funny noises but I never speak
I'm clever and know more than you'd think
I carry my young on my back, high and low
Hold tight, I tell them and don't let go

                  Can you find me?

I'm cute and I'm cuddly and a little bit round
And only in Australia can I be found
I lounge in the treetops of gum trees, you know
Eucalyptus they're called, silver bark, lovely smell
I sleep all day and eat all night
My diet is simple and plain
Leaves, leaves and more leaves the same
If you think it's boring then think again
The treetops are safe for most of the time
But now and again there are wild raging fires
A marsupial bear, in the outback I'm found
But live mainly in trees and not on the ground

Can you find me?

What bird can turn it's head right around?

If you have enjoyed my Riddly-Rhymes
And all the creatures, managed to find
I hope you've learnt a thing or two
Because I wrote them just for you
So when next you're feeling rather bored
Sit yourself down and read them once more

The End